TASMANIA
The Beautiful Island
Jennifer Pringle-Jones

Author: Jennifer Pringle-Jones

Publishers: Publishing House of Tasmania Pty Ltd

Distributor: Book Agencies of Tasmania,
65 Maluka Street, Bellerive, Tasmania
Ph. (002) 443177
Gary Allen Pty Ltd
9 Cooper Street, Smithfield, NSW
Ph. (02) 7252933

Photographs: Richard Bennett
Rob Blakers
Richard Eastwood
Chris Evenhuis
Owen Hughes
Malcolm Lindsay

Tourism Tasmania
Department of Lands, Parks & Wildlife
National Trust of Australia

Design: Brita Hansen

Printed in Hong Kong

c Jennifer Pringle-Jones

First published in 1989 by Publishing House of
Tasmania Pty Ltd, Hobart, Tasmania, Australia.

National Library of Australia
Cataloguing-in-Publication data

Pringle-Jones, Jennifer, 1946-
TASMANIA The Beautiful Island

ISBN 1 875210 00 8

Front cover: *Port Arthur Church (Richard Eastwood)*
Back cover: *Coles Bay (Tourism Tasmania)*
Front interior: *Near Longford (Owen Hughes)*
Back interior: *Workman's cottage, Entally House (Owen Hughes)*
Opposite: *Shot Tower, Taroona (Richard Eastwood)*

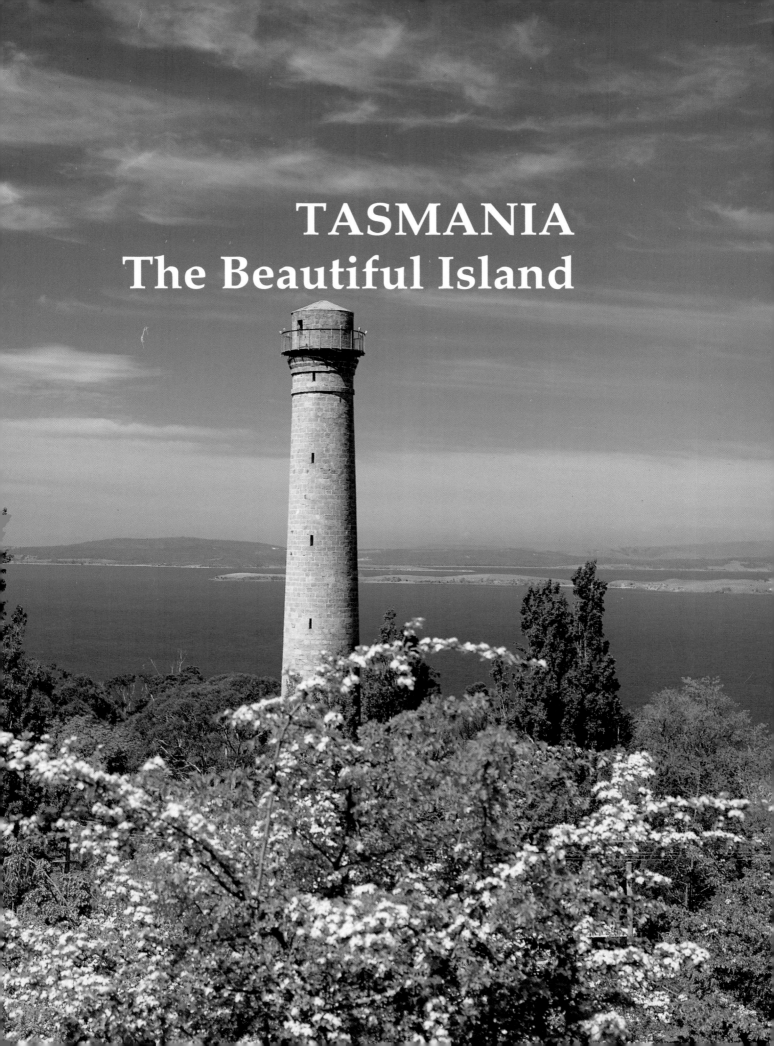

TASMANIA
The Beautiful Island

TASMANIA
The Beautiful Island

Jennifer Pringle-Jones

Publishing House of Tasmania

Beauty

When the waters of the Ice Age polar cap melted near the 40th parallel of latitude they left behind a heart-shaped island that is now called Tasmania.

Although it was formed about 12,000 years ago, it wasn't until 1798 that anyone proved it was separate from the bulk of the Australian continent. After setting out from Sydney, explorers George Bass and Matthew Flinders discovered a strait between the two land masses, and this 240 kilometre wide stretch of water between Tasmania and Victoria was named after Bass.

Originally known as Van Diemen's Land, Tasmania was the second Australian State settled by Europeans. However, in many respects, it has retained more of its historic links than many areas developed much later.

Country towns such as Bothwell, Richmond, Ross and Longford are like time capsules, and when locals dress in period costumes for events

such as the annual Evandale Village Fair they look just as much "at home" as their modern-day counterparts.

It would be wrong, though, to say that progress has by-passed Tasmania. Buildings constructed from the latest materials and utilising up-to-the-minute technology co-exist with sandstone Georgian structures, while the island leads the way in many forms of industrial development.

Disapproval of some earlier planning decisions has led to the formation of vocal community groups who join with authorities in ensuring that new projects are in keeping with natural and historic environs.

Tasmanian cities will never be bustling metropolises like Australia's larger centres. In reality, most people would prefer them to stay much the same as they are today. Hobart, Launceston, Burnie, Devonport, Glenorchy and Clarence have all the amenities of the "big smoke", but also have the advantage of short

distances between the population centres, general facilities and points of interest. One of the beauties of Tasmania is that peak hour traffic lasts less than 15 minutes! In recent times, it's been the more leisurely pace of life that has attracted both new settlers and visitors, many of whom want to escape the hurly burly and pace that go hand in hand with so many places these days.

The clean air and natural beauty are also drawcards, notably for people who regard this as an ideal environment in which to pursue art and craft work. Superb raw material, especially timber — much of which is found only in this State, are a bonus.

Tasmania harbours many riches in the land and in the surrounding seas. In addition to the natural resources such as minerals and timber there are the harvests cultivated by man — fruits, dairy products and vegetables, plus livestock that have put Tasmania on the world map as a producer of top-quality meat, hides and fleeces.

Both today and in the past, when Tasmania was solely the domain of aborigines, the inhabitants have looked to the sea as a source of food. Now, the local seafoods, notably the farmed salmon and trout, the abalone and other shellfish, are contributing to the island's growing reputation as a gourmet's paradise.

It's not only a paradise on the culinary front, though. From a scenic point of view, it's doubtful if any other place offers such a variety within a 68,000 square kilometre area. Majestic mountain ranges, trout-filled highland lakes, verdant pasturelands, craggy coastlines, tranquil bays and wilderness of world heritage status are just short distances apart.

The coastal and inland waterways, the wild rivers, rainforests and other wilderness areas provide adventure playgrounds that are unequalled in Australia.

Coupled with the natural beauty of both undeveloped and developed areas, the lifestyle of Tasmania makes this an ideal place to reflect on all the "good things in life".

P.6   *Grazing near Ben Lomond in the North-East*

P.7   *The Gunpowder Mill, Launceston, typifies modern man-made attractions based on an historic theme*

P.8   *Trigger plants, common in many parts of Tasmania, flourish high above Waterfall Bay on the East Coast*

P.9   *The Derwent Valley is a photographer's paradise, especially along the riverbank in Autumn*

Lifestyle

Tasmania is Australia's most decentralised State, with less than half the population in the metropolitan area of the capital, Hobart.

Most people live in coastal cities and towns and in farming districts, while the Central Plateau is sparcely populated and the South-West is only inhabited permanently by a handful of residents.

It's surprising in an island of only 450,000 people to find so many and such distinct regional differences. Initially, these largely came about because of physical barriers — mountains, forests and rivers, but, in time, the differing occupations and interests also tended to knit together people from certain areas.

There is no doubt that lifestyles vary between the mining centres of the West Coast, the agricultural districts of the North-West and

Midlands, the leisure resorts of the East Coast, the Central Plateau and the southern region. However, irrespective of where they live, most people agree that the quality of the lifestyle in Tasmania makes up for the quantity found in larger places.

Probably the greatest advocates for living in the island are those residents who are able to travel beyond their local shores, "re-charge", and then return to appreciate what this State has to offer.

A German couple who spent two years visiting different countries around the globe looking for what they considered to be the safest and most pleasant place to live and bring up children finally chose Hobart. No doubt they, too, where echoing the sentiments of renowned British photographer Lord Snowden, who declared during a visit to Tasmania that this is "the closest place to Heaven on Earth".

P.16 Sunset at Taranna in the South-East. Tasmania has long twilights, with daylight up to 9 pm in Summer.

P.18 The Nut at Stanley is a basalt formation that rises 120 metres from the sea to a plateau. There is a chairlift to the summit of this distinctive landmark.

P.19 Apple blossom in the Huon Valley. Tasmania is still referred to as the Apple Isle, and new varieties are being developed.

The Hobart Sheraton Hotel and Mures Fish Centre are among places serving superb ocean and farmed seafoods

P.20 Dairying and vegetable production are among the main industries of the lush North-West, which is also noted for timber production.

History

Internationally, the history of Australia since European settlement fills less than a page in a volume. When it comes to the national level, though, Tasmania figures prominently.

More of Australia's colonial heritage is preserved here than in other States and Territories. This is partly because the island's isolation has protected it to a certain extent from developers sweeping through and taking all in their path, and also because the locals have learnt lessons from those who demolished historic structures in other places settled early last century and later regretted this destruction.

Special attention has been paid to the need to preserve buildings and reminders of the activities of people from all walks of life — the humble as well as those in positions of authority. Just as much care has gone into the restoration of a miller's cottage at Richmond as into mansions like Clarendon at Nile and the superb collection of former warehouses in Salamanca Place, Hobart.

There are also about 16 classified historic towns, many of which are noted for specific structures — the intricately carved Ross Bridge, the bridge and churches in Richmond, the Callington Mill in Oatlands and Highfield at Stanley. Like Zeehan in the West, Swansea in the East, Deloraine in the North-West and Kempton in the South, they retain much of the atmosphere that existed more than 100 years ago.

It's trendy now to live in places like the former seafarers' village of Battery Point, near the Hobart city centre, and interstate buyers are among those acquiring historic properties in out-of-town centres such as Bothwell, Carrick, Campbell Town and Evandale, all within commuting distance of the main cities.

P.30   *Richmond Bridge, built in 1823, is the oldest still in use in Australia*
P.31   *A mail coach in an outbuilding at Entally House*
P.32   *The penitentiary at Port Arthur, the largest, but not the harshest, of the colonial penal settlements*

Building materials provide information about the development of particular regions. In the North-West, where timber was a readily available resource, many older buildings have fallen into disrepair or simply disappeared. By contrast, the solid sandstone blocks hewn from quarries at Orford, Pontville, on the shores of North-West Bay and many other places around the State still sit proudly in simple cottages and larger complexes like Anglesea Barracks, the Cascade Brewery, the Penny Royal, churches, inns and bridges. Bluestone was a favoured material on the East Coast, and bricks bearing the thumb imprint of convicts are found in many older buildings.

There are also recreated settings from the past. At Derby, in the North-East, cribshed tearooms, stores and a working mine revive the days when this was a bustling tin mining district. Port Arthur once again has a steam-powered bush mill and Swansea's bark mill is back in operation on the East Coast.

The colonial outposts of Port Arthur and Maria Island are among those with stark reminders of

the harsh days in the penal settlements. However, in a complete turnaround, visitors now stay voluntarily in the former penitentiary at Maria Island, and people are actually keen to step ashore at Sarah Island in Macquarie Harbour, the most dreaded of the penal establishments.

One of the most exciting recent tourism developments has been the opening up of historic properties for visitor accommodation. Now it's possible to experience at first hand what it was like to live in places as diverse as harbourmasters' cottages at Stanley and Strahan, the hospital of a convict outstation at Koonya on the Tasman Peninsula, a workman's cottage on a farm near Oatlands, a dispensary at Richmond, a post office at Lisdillon on the East Coast and an old bakery in Launceston.

More than 3,500 buildings and other structures are classified by the National Trust, which manages a number of properties that are open to the public. Clarendon, Entally House and Franklin House are in the North. Home Hill, once the residence of the only Tasmanian-born

Prime Minister of Australia, Sir Joseph Lyons, and Dame Enid Lyons, Australia's first woman cabinet member, is in the North-West, and Runnymede is in the Hobart suburb of New Town. With their traditional furnishings and attractive grounds they provide an insight into the gracious lifestyle of the more fortunate early settlers.

Other interesting properties include the Trust's southern headquarters in former Criminal Courts and the Penitentiary Chapel — a far cry from the past — and its northern information centre in an old umbrella shop!

Tasmanians are proud of their natural and historic heritage. They are keen to share these assets with visitors and are never too busy to fill them in with the well-known and lesser-known facts about what has "gone before".

P.34   St Andrew's Church, Evandale, dates from 1871. A village atmosphere still prevails in the township, noted for its old inns, colonial accommodation, art gallery, antique and craft establishments, plus a bakery specialising in old-fashioned loaves. Evandale turns back the clock each year when it hosts Penny farthing championships around the town.

P.35   Stables at Highfield near Stanley, where a large estate was established in the 1830s as headquarters for the Van Diemen's Land Company. Highfield is now owned by the Tasmanian Government, with buildings being preserved and restored including the elegant homestead. The complex is proving to be an important tourist attraction.

P.36   Bridge Street in Richmond, once the Granary of Van Diemen's Land. "Old" is a common, but treasured, word here. The old establishments include St John's Church, St Luke's Church, the gaol, the bridge, inns, tearooms, shops and, of course, the houses. Richmond is very much a town of a by-gone era.

P.37   The dining room at Runnymede, a National Trust property in the northern Hobart suburb of New Town. Regency-style Runnymede was built in 1840 by Robert Pitcairn, one of the first lawyers to qualify in Tasmania. A bishop and a shipowner were among other early owners. The stables, coachhouse and delightful gardens are also open to the public.

P.38 The former Commandant's house at Port
      Arthur occupies a prime site overlooking the
      bay. This was a penal settlement from
      1830-1877. Now it is managed by the
      Department of Lands, Parks and Wildlife,
      which is progressively restoring many of the
      key settlement buildings.

P.40 Clarendon, at Nile, was one of Australia's
      finest Georgian residences. Built by James
      Cox in 1838, it is now owned by the National
      Trust. Antiques and classic furnishings
      complement this outstanding property, which
      is set in extensive parklands.

P.41 A quiet stillness pervades Saltwater River,
      once a penal outstation and coal mining
      centre on the Tasman Peninsula. Only the
      ruins remain to tell the story of the convicts
      sent here to what was referred to as "hell on
      earth".

      Ross Bridge is noted for its superb
      carvings—the work of convicts Daniel
      Herbert and James Colbeck. Other links with
      the past at Ross include colonial buildings
      and a Wool Centre.

Leisure

The four distinct seasons in Tasmania foster diverse pursuits, but the island's greatest asset is that so many unrelated activities can be undertaken within close proximity of each other.

Joggers running along Nutgrove Beach, just 3 kilometres from the Hobart GPO, can glance up to the snow-clad Mount Wellington, towering 1,271 metres above the city; likewise, the yachtsmen and women who make the most of the broad expanses of the River Derwent for year-round competitive and pleasure sailing.

With no part of Tasmania more than 115 kilometres from the sea, there's a natural tendency towards boating, canoeing, fishing, surfing, windsurfing, kayaking, diving, swimming and general water-based recreation. The same situation applies inland, where rafting on wild rivers like the Franklin in the West or the quieter reaches of the Picton in the South, and trout fishing — especially in the thousands of highland lakes, are among the activities that are luring visitors from many parts of the world.

Nutgrove Beach, Sandy Bay
Launceston, the "Garden City"

The East Coast resorts of St Helens, Coles Bay, Bicheno, Swansea and Orford are particularly popular during the Summer, and here, as in other parts of the State, daylight saving between October and March ensures that in mid-Summer it's still light as late as 9 pm. Long twilight hours are a feature of the island at most times of the year.

When Tasmanians head off to their holiday homes it may be only a 20-minute journey, but the transition south from Hobart to Coningham, for instance, is a journey to a world of bushland, State reserves, sandy coves, unpolluted beaches and the superb waterways of North-West Bay and the D'Entrecasteaux Channel. In the North, Greens Beach and other Tamar River resorts are just a short drive from Tasmania's second largest city, Launceston, and on the North-West Coast, Boat Harbour and Hawley Beach are also within close commuting distance of the cities.

Snow skiing is a growth Winter sport, the main centres being Ben Lomond, 64 kilometres south-east of Launceston, and Mt. Field, 75 kilometres west of Hobart. The season usually lasts from July to September, and although the slopes are not as developed as in mainland

Australian resorts, they, too, have the advantage of being close to main population centres.

Golf is a year-round favourite, and there are club and public courses in most parts of the State. Lawn bowls is another popular pursuit.

With more than 914,000 ha of Tasmania in national parks there are obviously plenty of opportunities for bushwalking, photography, and, for the more adventurous, abseiling and even hang gliding.

You don't have to be "sporty" to enjoy Tasmania, however. Three-quarters of the State is traversed by highways and byways, with plenty of idyllic spots for picnics or "just watching the world go by".

Public parks and gardens combining native and introduced species are another favourite visiting spot. From cottage plantings to the vast expanses of the Royal Tasmanian Botanical Gardens, Tasmania is noted for the bright colours of its flowers, which are not subjected to the humidity and heat experienced in many other parts of Australia.

For viewing of another kind, the various codes of football, horse racing, greyhound racing and cricket are among the most popular spectator sports.

World-class sporting venues include the picturesque Lake Barrington rowing course near Sheffield in the North-West, while yachting puts Tasmania in the international spotlight each year during the classic Sydney to Hobart Yacht Race and the associated Melbourne to Hobart and Melbourne to Devonport races. Hobart's waterfront is at its busiest as the yachts complete their journeys and the docks become the scene of countless parties, sporting and cultural events, including special showings of Tasmania's outstanding art and crafts.

In fact, one of the more pleasurable ways of spending leisure hours at any time of the year is to visit the many outlets featuring locally produced paintings, prints, timber products, pottery, glassware, leather goods and clothing made from Tasmanian wool, cashmere and mohair.

P.44   *Waterman's Dock on the Hobart waterfront*

Devonport has a particularly picturesque golf course

P.45   *Highland lakes are a mecca for trout fishing enthusiasts*

P.46   *The 1825 Penny Royal cornmill, Launceston*

P.47   *Surfing near Wedge Island, in the South-East*

The Royal Tasmanian Botanical Gardens, a Hobart showpiece

P.48 *Bicheno, at the centre of the Sunshine Coast in the East, has been a haven for seafarers - first the sealers and whalers and, now, the fishermen.*

P.50 *Wineglass Bay near Coles Bay is a vista of long white, sandy beaches and clear aqua water. Naturally, it's a favoured spot for pursuits such as boating, diving and swimming.*

P.51   The Cascade Brewery - Australia's oldest -
        stands like a sentinel in South Hobart.
        Visitors can tour the brewery and the
        company's large garden with its old-fashioned
        roses and massive rhododendrons.
        The Victorian Gallery in the Tasmanian
        Museum and Art Gallery, Hobart, is the
        setting for displays of 19th century paintings,
        sculpture and furniture. It's even a 19th
        century building!

P.52   Pleasure craft now ply Macquarie Harbour,
        the waters of which once carried the vessels
        delivering convicts to the dreaded Sarah
        Island settlement. The port of Strahan is
        nearby.

Wilderness

South-western Tasmania is one of the world's last temperate wilderness areas. It includes open buttongrass plains, dense eucalypt forests, mountain moors and undisturbed coastal scenery. Some of it is impenetrable; in other sections walkers trek where aborigines roamed thousands of years ago. Evidence of their existence, including rock paintings and tools, has been found in a number of recently discovered caves.

They provide just a few of the examples of the earth's evolutionary history that is captured in the South-West, an area that was accorded world heritage status in 1982.

The Western Tasmania Wilderness National Parks World Heritage Area consists of the Cradle Mountain/Lake St. Clair National Park, the Franklin/Lower Gordon Wild Rivers National Park and the South-West National Park.

Abrupt weather changes are common in the wilderness areas, and in the South-West it rains about 200 days each year. As a result, the best times for bushwalking are between October and April.

Flights in light aircraft make the South-West accessible to those with less time or fortitude!

Other places, too, can be explored more easily than in the past. The use of four-wheel drive vehicles on timber trails and pioneer tracks, especially on the West Coast, has opened up regions that were previously the domain of only the hardiest trekkers.

For generations the overland track through the Cradle Mountain/Lake St. Clair National Park in the western highlands has been a favourite with visitors from near and far. They come here to experience the exhilaration of walking through dense rainforests and moorlands flanked by windswept, craggy mountains, deep gorges, lakes, tarns and waterfalls.

Tasmania's wilderness is a world apart — a place where time stands still and man can truly communicate with nature.

P.54   The spectacular Franklin Gorge near the Fincham Track

P.55   Road's end - Dove Lake near Cradle Mountain

P.56   The Meander River wends its way from the Central Highlands through forests and grazing areas and on beyond the township of Deloraine

P.58   Barn Bluff is about six hours' walk away from the northern entrance to the Cradle Mountain/Lake St Clair National Park. Privately operated, self-contained chalets now add to the comfort of walkers trekking the famous Overland Track.

P.59   Port Davey is a point of entry to the south-west wilderness for people arriving by air or sea. The port, which was discovered by whaler/explorer Captain James Kelly in 1815, is a haven for bushwalkers.

Snow is common in the Central Highlands during Winter, but weather in Tasmania's wilderness areas can change without warning at any time

P.60 Weld River rainforest. The South-West, with
      its mountains, rain forests and buttongrass
      plains is a paradise for the more adventurous
      bushwalkers. However, others can also
      experience some of the magic from places such
      as Lake Pedder.

P.61 The Liffey Falls are in the geographic centre
      of Tasmania, sometimes referred to as the
      "heart" of the island. Other falls that are
      easily accessible include Russell Falls in the
      Mount Field National Park.

      Tasmania's waratahs are flatter and shorter
      than those found in mainland Australia, but
      they are just as eye-catching. Presumably the
      township of Waratah was named after the
      blooms because this is one of the areas where
      they are plentiful. They also flank tracks near
      Lake St Clair.

Islands of the Island

Tasmanians are rightfully offended when their State is left off the map of Australia. Imagine then the feelings of residents of Tasmania's off-shore islands when they are forgotten by their own mainland. From wind-swept Maatsuyker Island in the far South to King and Flinders Islands in Bass Strait, these land masses are characterised by both rugged and tranquil beauty.

They have played an important role in the exploration and development of Tasmania, providing vital links in communication networks and fostering valuable primary production.

Australia's most southerly lighthouse, at tiny Maatsuyker Island, has been a welcome sight for navigators for the past 100 years. Sea access to the island is very difficult and supplies for the two-man communications station are flown in by helicopter.

The station is an important weather monitoring base, with three-hourly reports being made to the Bureau of Meteorology.

There's also an historic lighthouse at Bruny Island, which is virtually two islands joined by a narrow isthmus. Livestock, seafood and timber are among Bruny's bountiful harvest, while visitors view the short sea crossing from Kettering as a route to a land of leisure pursuits such as coastal walking, diving and surfing.

Maria Island, off the East Coast, is a haven for holidaymakers and wildlife. Managed by the Department of Lands, Parks and Wildlife, this former penal settlement is now a fauna reserve, with Cape Barren geese, wallabies and emus quite at home among the day-trippers and campers.

The largest of the Bass Strait islands, King and Flinders, "stand guard" at the western and eastern ends of Tasmania's northern sea divide.

King Island is like a green oasis in the Strait, the lush pasturelands providing feed for beef cattle, sheep and the cows that produce the creamy milk used in the island's famous cheeses and other dairy products.

As with most Tasmanian islands, the locals turn to the sea for a plentiful supply of seafoods, notably crayfish and abalone. These can be treacherous waters, however, and the many shipwrecks around the shores point to the danger.

Flinders Island, the largest in the Furneaux Group, is a photographer's dream. The towering granite peak of Mt. Strzelecki, long, sandy beaches, sheltered lagoons and vast expanses of seemingly endless sea are all worth "capturing".

The island is steeped in history — from the days of the sealers and whalers to the time when this was the setting for an attempt to save the remnants of the full-blooded Tasmanian tribal people, and, now, to its more peaceful role as a popular holiday resort, a fishing and farming community.

All these islands are just as worthy of discovery as the rest of Tasmania.

P.62 *Projects on Maria Island include the restoration of buildings at Darlington and further development of the fauna reserve*

P.63 *Maatsuyker Island is an important communications base*

P.64 *(Top) Superb cruising waters surround Bruny Island*
(Bottom) From the mutton birds to the windmills, Flinders Island has a character all of its own. There are poignant reminders of the past, but it's also a place of contentment.

P.65 *Crayfish are among the fruits of the sea at King Island, while the lush green pastures are said to have developed from the seeds in straw mattresses washed ashore from shipwrecks.*